# How to Sell This Pen
Marketing of the Salesman

## Table of Contents

**Introduction** ............................................................ 4
   So what makes a Salesman ........................................... 7
   How to Sell ............................................................... 9

**Know Your Product** .................................................. 10
   Product Description ................................................. 11
   Using the Product Description .................................. 12
   Know Your Product to Sell Anything .......................... 13

**Be Persuasive** .......................................................... 14
   How to Persuade Your Consumers ............................ 15
   Be Persuasive to Sell Anything .................................. 18
   Influence People In Your Favor .................................. 20
   The Study of the Con Art .......................................... 24

**Know how People Think** ........................................... 28
   Cognitive Biases, Consumer Mind and Marketing ..... 28
   Know how People Think to Sell Anything ................. 35

**Treat Costumers Well** ............................................... 37
   Build Amazing Relationships .................................... 38
   Relationship Marketing with Your Target Audience .. 39
   Ideas for Relationship Marketing ............................. 41

**Be Trustworthy** ........................................................ 44
   Warranty or Risk Reversal ........................................ 45
   Your Credibility ....................................................... 47

**So, How to Sell this Pen** ........................................... 49

# Introduction

At the last chapter of this book you will learn how to sell this pen. (the pen on the cover of this book).
It goes like in the movie 300, when King Leonidas asks a bunch of people what they do. We could ask marketers what they do and the answers would be diverse:
- I prepare marketing campaigns
- I create brands
- I position brands
-       I do Marketing strategy
- I create ads and follow up on those ads to understand the metrics so that I can create even better ad campaigns.

Now if we ask a salesman what he does, he just answers AHWUUU.
- I sell.

That is pretty much what a salesman does, he sells. You hire a marketing team and they don't have to guarantee sales, at least not right away, it may take some time to position your brand, they may need to do some AB testing, or study the market and all other sciency things that make up marketing, because marketing is a science, and not a simple one, marketing is rocket science, it is complex and it covers many topics. If you want to be a master of marketing you should go to college, and study it there for 4 years, or 8 years, then you can say that you know marketing.

When you hire a salesman or a team of salesman they have to guarantee a certain number of sales, because that is what they do, they sell.

Of course I am downplaying things here, and selling is also a science, but it is not rocket science, people have been selling pretty much the same way for millennia, an 1875 man would know a modern day salesman by the time he would lay his eyes on him. It is the same art.

Selling is not marketing, selling is more like conning someone. And I don't mean that in the wrong way, being persuaded to do something is not always bad.

Selling is persuasion.

But the good news is that you don't need to spend 8 years in college to sell, you need to know some basic rules of selling, that given how current obsession with marketing we are calling marketing of the salesman, but could also be techniques of the salesman. You need to know this techniques to be able to sell anything (most things), including a pen.

## So what makes a Salesman

A salesman will have this characteristics:
1. **He knows the product** very well, but very well indeed.
2. **He is persuasive**, he talks like a salesman, which means he is assertive, well spoken, persuasive, friendly, well dressed, good presentation, no matter the age he just looks like he is in his prime
3. **He knows how people think**, he is manipulative, he is a con artist of sorts (he knows how people operate psychological)
4. **He Treats Costumers Well**, he gets to know you, he befriends you, he is charming because he is confident, it feels like you need him and not the contrary, and when he doesn't make the sell today, he couldn't care less, like there are other 10 people coming to buy from him. It looks like he is doing you a favor.
5. **He is Trustworthy**, after the sale you go home, and the product behaves exactly the way he told you it would. And the things he said about the product, like how the product will help you or make your life better, everything checked out, so much so, that he becomes a part of your enjoyment of the product, you think about

him while you use the product, he is that good. He is that trustworthy. You can't wait to buy from him again. He is your friend, not just someone who sold you a product. He is someone you need in your life, you want to, you need to buy from him Even if you have other opportunities to buy what he is offering you wait and buy from him, because you trust him, because he is an authority in his business, because he knows what he is talking about, because you are afraid to buy from anyone else. Because in a way you want that buy experience that he provides, you are willing to pay more for it, the way he talks to you, the way he makes you try other products, you kind of fall in love with him and nobody can replace him.

## How to Sell

1. Know your product
2. Be Persuasive
3. Know how People Think
4. Treat Costumers Well
5. Be trustworthy

Let's go through every single one of this items. You have to become good at every single one of them if you want to have more sales.

# Know Your Product

If you are selling something you should be the most fanatic user of that thing, or in case you can't be in constant company of people who are fanatic users of that thing.

You should have read everything there is to read about the product you are selling.

You should make a habit of reading the product brochure before going to sleep.

You should organize your knowledge about the product in the following categories:

## Product Description

A product description is a description that informs about product features, technologies, characteristics and other relevant information that will make the user most likely to buy the product. So it would be the sale points of the product, what about this product makes users **need** to buy it. To be more effective it **should focus on benefits of the product to end users**.

A product description is everything that is good, juicy and true about a product. Of course a product will have many features, but product descriptions focus on features that define the product on user's mind and set them apart from competing products.

## Using the Product Description

The Product Description is just the first part you need to talk about the product. You will also have to take a look at product descriptions from competing products on the same category and compare them favorably to the product you are selling.

You will have to be familiar with the entire industry your product is in, and where that industry is heading, the more information you have about the product, competing products and the industry the better salesman you will be.

## Know Your Product to Sell Anything

Even if you will are not a salesman and just want to sell a book, a website subscription, or an online product in general you should use the tactics that salesmen use.
So first you should write a product description of your product, in the most eloquent way you can. Talking about it from an authoritative point of view. And then you should get informative about products in the same category as yours and then add to your product description comparing your product to the industry and to competing products. This is an opportunity for you to show your authority, knowledge and competence in the business you are. You should be familiar with all competing products and the industry and you should show it in your copy. The costumer must be able to read your product description and feel your authority, competence, experience and broad knowledge of the subject. And you should do it eloquently. Don't try to keep it short, your costumer is about to pay for your service or product, give him the description that the product deserves, if it is just 30 seconds, that is good, but if it requires 2 minutes, that is fine too.

So you will display the same knowledge of the product that a salesman would. This will be your marketing strategy.

## Be Persuasive

Being persuasive means being able to cause people to do or believe in something. To do that you must have good reasoning and you should be assertive. You should use the right terms, you must be confident, you should show results.

# How to Persuade Your Consumers

The Six Principles of Influence (also known as Six Weapons of Influence) were created by Robert Cialdini, Emeritus Professor of Regents of Psychology and Marketing at Arizona State University. He published them in his respected 1984 book "Influence: The Psychology of Persuasion".

The six principles are as follows:

**1. Reciprocity**

As humans, we generally aim to return favors, pay back debts, and treat others as they treat us. According to the idea of reciprocity, this can lead us to feel obliged to offer concessions or discounts to others if they have offered them to us. This is because we're uncomfortable with feeling indebted to them.

For example, if a colleague helps you when you're busy with a project, you might feel obliged to support her ideas for improving team processes. You might decide to buy more from a supplier if they have offered you an aggressive discount. Or, you might give money to a charity fundraiser who has given you a flower in the street.

## 2. Commitment (and Consistency)

Cialdini says that we have a deep desire to be consistent. For this reason, once we've committed to something, we're then more inclined to go through with it.

For instance, you'd probably be more likely to support a colleague's project proposal if you had shown interest when he first talked to you about his ideas.

## 3. Social Proof

This principle relies on people's sense of "safety in numbers."

For example, we're more likely to work late if others in our team are doing the same, put a tip in a jar if it already contains money, or eat in a restaurant if it's busy. Here, we're assuming that if lots of other people are doing something, then it must be OK.

We're particularly susceptible to this principle when we're feeling uncertain, and we're even more likely to be influenced if the people we see seem to be similar to us. That's why commercials often use moms, not celebrities, to advertise household products.

## 4. Liking

Cialdini says that we're more likely to be influenced by people we like. Likability comes in many forms – people might be similar or familiar to us, they might give us compliments, or we may just simply trust them.

Companies that use sales agents from within the community employ this principle with huge success. People are more likely to buy from people like themselves, from friends, and from people they know and respect.

### 5. Authority

We feel a sense of duty or obligation to people in positions of authority. This is why advertisers of pharmaceutical products employ doctors to front their campaigns, and why most of us will do most things that our manager requests.

Job titles, uniforms, and even accessories like cars or gadgets can lend an air of authority, and can persuade us to accept what these people say.

### 6. Scarcity

This principle says that things are more attractive when their availability is limited, or when we stand to lose the opportunity to acquire them on favorable terms.

For instance, we might buy something immediately if we're told that it's the last one, or that a special offer will soon expire.

## Be Persuasive to Sell Anything

You shouldn't try to implement all six principles of influence in ever one of your marketing efforts. But they should be second nature to you and you should summon them when you need it. And you can only do that if you understand what the six principles are.

Reciprocity is very simple. If you are good to me, I will be good to you. If you offer free advice to people, they will feel obliged to buy from you. You shouldn't be afraid to be the good guy in business because people will be rooting for you. People will support you.

Commitment is about getting your client to take a small step in order to later get him to take a bigger step. Commitment comes in many forms like free trial, discounts for new users, serialized products and more.

Social Proof is about your numbers. How many clients have you helped with your product.

Liking is something that is just in our nature. We want people we buy from to be just like us, so we can fantasize that they have the same problems we do.

Authority is a must if you want to persuade people. People who buy from you should look at you and see experience, knowledge and competence personified. You should talk about the products you sell like you are obsessed. Like you live for them.

Scarcity is about showing that your product is so valuable it is flowing from the shelves. Everybody wants what is popular. That is why there will always be a top category.

# Influence People In Your Favor

**Names**

Use a person's name, or their title depending on the situation.

Dale Carnegie, the author of *How to Win Friends and Influence People*, believed that using someone's name was incredibly important. He said that a person's name is the sweetest sound in any language for that person.

Difficult though it is, if you can get into the habit of not only remembering someone's name when you first meet them, but using their name in the subsequent conversation, they'll find you terribly charming and wonderful.

**Mirroring**

Mirror their behavior.

Mirroring people's body language when you interact with them is a way of building up trust. Just be subtle about it.

Repeating something that another person says, and copying his gestures in a mild way, often establishes a comforting relationship for the other person towards you. Repeating his words makes him believe that he is being listened to and he has your attention.

**Door-in-the-Face Technique**
CHILD: Grandma, can I have a whole pizza?
YOU: What? No.
CHILD: How about just one cookie?
YOU: One cookie coming up, kid.

There is a trick if you want a big favor, first ask for a bigger one. Much bigger. When your opponent refuses he will have the guilty feeling that he owes you at least a smaller favor.
It is also called Contrasting. Contrasting is the technique where you demand much higher than what you actually want, and eventually bargain down to exactly what you wanted in the first place. It has been a highly effective technique, and is used quite often by many people. Human thinking is not absolute. We think of things in relation. And so, this technique works because of the contrasting difference of scale it creates in the mind of the other person. They feel a bit harsh themselves when they reject your initial unrealistic request, and jump right in at the next one that seems relatively doable.

**Foot-in-the-Door Technique**

The Foot-in-the-Door Technique is the opposite of Door-in-the-Face, but equally as effective. In this situation, you start small, and go big. In other words, you ask someone to do a simple job. They do it. Having created a sense of obligation, you can now make a much bigger request from that person.

**Give 2 Options**
To get someone to make a decision, offer them a choice of two options. It will keep them from being overwhelmed, and give them a sense of control.

**Nontrivial vocabulary**
When we use special terminology, we intentionally make our opponent's intellectual status lower. The opponent might feel severe discomfort due to his own incompetence. To break his confidence completely, try to quote famous people. Now you can direct the conversation in any direction you want.

**Be Polite**

The words 'thank you' and 'please' are magic words of persuasion. If you recall from your own experiences, you will definitely remember instances where you were able to persuade people by a simple combination of a smiling face and the word 'please'. We all are taught and conditioned this way from childhood. Humans are pretty much used to reacting to these gestures in a particular way. We tend to be more open towards requests, rather than instructions. Sugarcoat these requests with polite expressions and you'll at least have your request considered, if not accepted.

**Do Not Force People**
When people feel that their freedom to choose an action is threatened, they get an unpleasant feeling called 'reactance'. This also motivates them to perform the threatened behavior, thus proving that their free will has not been compromised.

Beware of persuading too overtly or too much. If people get wind that they are being railroaded, they will leap right off the tracks.

## The Study of the Con Art

Con Artist are sales people turned bad, but we can benefit from knowing how they operate. We will not use our knowledge for evil, but knowing how people can easily be manipulated will help us better serve them. And it also shows some of Caldini's science in action.

This is an extract from a BBC story about Con Artists:
The research has identified a number of characteristics that people who are victims of scams seem to share in common. Some of these traits – like a lack of self-control – we would probably recognise as dangerous. But others – a trust in authority, a desire to act in the same way as our friends, or a tendency to act in a consistent way – we might think of as good characteristics.

These may be new findings to psychologists, but they are not new to scammers. Modic points out, for instance, that some scammers gain a victim's trust by pretending to share a mutual friend. In other situations the scammer might contact the victim under the guise of a figure of authority – a doctor or a lawyer - to appear more persuasive. There are also scams that initially involve no loss of money and which are designed to encourage a victim to behave in a certain way, so that later they are more likely to behave in the same way when their money is at stake.Some card game swindles use this strategy.

scammers repeatedly used one or more of the same seven persuasion principles. Three of these principles are similar to those Modic identified by talking to potential or actual scam victims. Scammers use the "time principle" to persuade us we need to act quickly before we can think rationally and exercise self-control. They also make use of the "deference to authority principle" and the "herd principle" – our tendency to act like our friends or those around us – to convince people that the scam is legitimate.

There's a good reason for that, he says: many of the vulnerabilities that scammers exploit are actually human strengths rather than weaknesses. He points to the work of psychologist Robert Cialdini at Arizona State University, who is famous for his work on the psychology of persuasion. "He's explained that the authority principle, for example, is actually very helpful for surviving peacefully in human society," says Stajano. "We shouldn't see scam victims as stupid – they're acting in a way that's beneficial for our survival most of the time."

End of Article.

The confidence game — the con — is an exercise in soft skills. Trust, sympathy, persuasion. The true con artist doesn't force us to do anything; he makes us complicit in our own undoing. He doesn't steal. We give. He doesn't have to threaten us. We supply the story ourselves. We believe because we want to, not because anyone made us. And so we offer up whatever they want — money, reputation, trust, fame, legitimacy, support — and we don't realize what is happening until it is too late. Our need to believe, to embrace things that explain our world, is as pervasive as it is strong. Given the right cues, we're willing to go along with just about anything and put our confidence in just about anyone.

salespeople signal to our brains that everything is as it should be. Their smooth behavior raises our confidence, thereby boosting our serotonin levels. The well-being chemical serotonin can turn off our critical sense and increase our feeling of content — so much so that our initial beliefs never are subjected to scrutiny in the vmPFC, and the anterior insula never gives us the warning sign that would make us step back and think.

It is perfectly natural that we fall victim to the confidence tricks of scam artists. Our brains were not hardwired to look through the clever schemes and confidence-installing tricks of skilled actors and con men trained in making our disbelief go away. Our gray matter can distinguish honesty from dishonesty and alarming situations from unruffled ones but it cannot instinctively detect dishonesty and fraud cleverly disguised.

# Know how People Think

To understand how people think we must take a look at cognitive biases.

## Cognitive Biases, Consumer Mind and Marketing

Cognitive biases are the tendencies to think in certain ways that can lead to systematic drifts of logic and irrational decisions. Or on the other are the rules that dictate the functioning of the human mind. Let us look at some of these rules of human behavior and by extension of consumer behavior:

**Ambiguity Effect**
The tendency to avoid options for which missing information makes the probability seem "unknown."
*Use in Marketing*: If a user doesn't understand your product or a particular choice, he will not choose it. People tend to avoid the unknown. Make sure the information about your product is clear and plentiful, if necessary, create leaflets.

**Anchoring or Focalism**

The tendency to rely too heavily, or "anchor," on one trait or piece of information when making decisions (usually the first piece of information that we acquire on that subject)

*Use in Marketing*: The price of the first product (or information) you give your customer will set expectations for him to evaluate the subsequent products, what the customer's mind does not realize is that you created the price of the first product in the first place but even so he relies too much in it and uses it in comparison with your other prices. Apple in the picture below says the first phone costs $ 99, you will use this price as a basis to evaluate the price of the second and third handset.

**Confirmation Bias**

The tendency to search for, interpret, focus on and remember information in a way that confirms one's preconceptions. We tend to listen only to information that confirms our prejudices.
*Use in Marketing* - Improve the effectiveness of your marketing, adjusting a product with prejudices and expectations of the target audience. For example if you are going to sell wine use a bottle of wine that is expected by the target audience. But use this tactic with caution, sometimes you can be successful surprising the audience with something they did not expect.

**Availability Cascade**
A self-reinforcing process in which a collective belief gains more and more plausibility through its increasing repetition in public discourse (or "repeat something long enough and it will become true").
*Use in Marketing*: When your website, brand, or product is referenced repeatedly by others, people are more likely to think highly of it. The more social buzz you generate, the better. When you do your marketing campaigns you can repeat the campaign several times even if it is for the same target audience. There is a saying in marketing: "The first time a man sees your ad, he ignores it. The second he pays attention. The third time he talks about your ad with his wife. The fourth he's ready to buy. "

## Bandwagon Effect

The tendency to do (or believe) things because many other people do (or believe) the same. Related to groupthink and herd behavior.

*Use in Marketing*: Improve your marketing effectiveness by showing past sales numbers (if they are significant), even better if your product is the best seller (best rated, most lended, etc.). For example nothing makes a book sell more than being on the bestseller list.

## Base Rate Fallacy

The tendency to ignore base rate information (generic, general information) and focus on specific information (information only pertaining to a certain case).

*Use in Marketing*: Do not just share information about your product - annoying statistics, pictures, resources, etc. Instead, show how your product works in specific examples. Use case studies and testimonials from users. Even large multinationals like Microsoft, Apple do.

## Belief Bias

An effect where someone's evaluation of the logical strength of an argument is biased by the believability of the conclusion.

*Use in Marketing*: When persuading users to buy your product, show them how it will help them. The personal positive result of them using the product is going to trump your argument as to why it's so good.

**Choice-supportive Bias**
The tendency to remember one's choices as better than they actually were.
*Use in Marketing*: If your customer makes a choice, praise them. They will forever think that they made the right choice. Congratulate them on their purchase. Very used in restaurants where no matter what wine the customer chooses the waiter goes: "excellent choice".

**Clustering Illusion**
This is the tendency to see patterns in random events.
*Use in Marketing*: If you want to persuade your users, focus on the qualities that put your product or service in the best light and ignore those that may be detrimental. But of course use with limits, a bad product should absolutely not be sold.

**Confirmation bias**
The tendency to prefer information that confirms one's beliefs or hypotheses, whether or not they are true.

*Use in Marketing*: you will have a hard time changing the user's prejudices. Instead, try to connect with them on an emotional level, and do everything you can to explore their prejudices in your own benefit.

**Conjunction Fallacy**
The tendency to assume that specific conditions are more probable than general ones.
*Use in Marketing*: Use customer testimonials. Specific conditions and examples always trump general explanations and data.

**Conservatism**
The tendency to revise one's belief insufficiently when presented with new evidence.
*Use in Marketing*: Your presentation of the product or service alone is not persuasive. Use charts, present numbers, metrics, statistical data, you should strengthen your persuasive power not only with emotional argumentation but also with alternative forms of persuasion.

**Contrast Effect**
The enhancement or reduction of a certain perception's stimuli when compared with a recently observed, contrasting object.

*Use in Marketing*: Make your product stand out as much as possible. Using surprise, differentiation and shock value, you can make your product more memorable and therefore more likely to be bought by people.

**Zero-risk Bias**
Sociologists have found that we love certainty — even if it's counter productive.
*Use in Marketing*: Improve the effectiveness of marketing by presenting a product or service as risk-free. Offer guarantees.

**Survivorship Bias**
An error that comes from focusing only on surviving examples, causing us to misjudge a situation.
*Use in Marketing*: Improve marketing effectiveness by focusing on positive results (regardless of whether the product has produced them).

**Recency Effect**
The tendency to weigh the latest information more heavily than older data.
*Use in Marketing*: Improve marketing effectiveness by controlling the last message your customer sees about your product, often at the point of sale, such as labeling in the package or product descriptions online.

**Overconfidence Effect**
People are too confident about their abilities, and this causes them to take greater risks in their daily lives.
*Use in Marketing*: Increase marketing effectiveness by presenting a product as helping to achieve goals or ambitions of unlikely but desired goals.

# Know how People Think to Sell Anything

Most salesman can't name 2 cognitive biases, but they use it everyday. Because before the science, these cognitive biases occur in nature, in everyday life. A salesman takes a look at you and knows how to sell you the product he is selling.
How?
He is looking at everything about you:
- How are you dressed
- Do you have a watch
- What kind of shoes you wear
- Are you clumsy or not

He is sherlocking you.
And the next thing that comes of his mouth:

- Hi, you look like you could use a new iron.

And here he talks about the day to day life of this particular costumer like he knows him, talks about how this new steam iron could facilitate his life. All from observing. Studying people is the result of trial and error not only the knowledge of cognitive biases. After three seconds talking to someone you can tell if you can turn the person in a buyer or not. It comes with experience.

To sell anything you must go through trial and error, you must optimize your product and the selling experience, doing lots of A, B testing. One week you test the website like this, and the other week you test it like that.

You have to study your costumer; you have to be obsessed with your costumers.

# Treat Costumers Well

You must serve your costumer.

You must be passionate about making your costumer happy.

You must be polite, but are the same time take some initiative. You must be truthfully and honest without hurting your costumer's feelings. Help him be a better version of himself with your product.

You must satiate your costumer's needs.

When a costumer comes to talk to you, you face should look like that just made your day.

Treating him well should be your absolute priority not getting his money. He may not buy today, but he feels like he is loved, respected, and hold in high regard, he will come back, because that feels incredibly good, to be the object of someone's respect and undivided attention.

But all of this has to be natural, you shouldn't have to force it. The first thing you must do is fall in love with your industry and your products. If you love them, you will love your costumers even more.

You must build relationships.

# Build Amazing Relationships

Your friends may be your future business partners.
Your costumers make great friends and you can build lasting business relationships with them. Nobody makes it on their own, friendships are very important.
The first thing you need to make friends is Great Education of course. We get money by solving people's problems. If you are for example a mechanic but didn't spend enough time getting better, learning the trade and you are not a master and have no intention of becoming one, you will never be able to provide great service, and your costumers will know. But if you invested in your education, learned to assembly and disassembly different cars, you are familiar with all major car brands and always pay attention to new parts or news from the manufacturers, than you will be a master at what you do, and you will be extremely competent, an authority in your field, your clients will be very pleased with your service, and there will be plenty of opportunities to great and lasting relationships with people that will help you succeed and that will be there for you, when you need to get that loan to open a shop.

# Relationship Marketing with Your Target Audience

You must build relationships with customers because repeat purchases make a large part of the capital that goes into any company and because it is much easier to convince someone who has already bought from you before.

Why do most companies lose customers? Poor service? Yes. Poor quality? Yes. And why else? Apathy after the sale. Most companies lose customers by ignoring them to death.

Mistaken businessman think that marketing is over as soon as they make the sale.

Marketing begins as soon as you make the sale. It is of great importance for you and your company, that you understand this.

It is six times more expensive to sell a product to a new customer than to an existing customer. There are businesses that, after one or two years garnering customers, survive, pay their bills, and grow entirely thanks to those customers the company already has and to whom the company directs its Marketing acts.

Furthermore, if you maintain a relationship with your customers, it will be easier for you to know what products they buy and like even long after the sale and what other products your customers like that you can introduce, they can even be from another industry, thereby helping you to diversify your entrepreneurship initiatives.
Customer retention is important because:

1. It costs less to serve long-term customers.
2. Loyal customers will pay a price premium.
3. Loyal customers will generate word-of-mouth referrals to other prospective customers.

# Ideas for Relationship Marketing

Relationship Marketing is simple, you just have to be friends with your customers, which is easy because they are what sustain your business and are your reason to exist.
Let's look at some ways to keep in touch with your customers:

**Newsletter and Email**
Newsletters can be either via email or printed, they contain information about your new products, prices and promotions. It may also be a way for you to inform your clients about your company's news, what activities you have been doing, and about what charity events or sponsorships you have been involved with.
Always leave a page of the Newsletter dedicated to information on how you can be contacted.
Nowadays the best way to do Newsletters is from the internet, through email with services like MailChimp that manage your emails. You can collect emails from your customers after a purchase, but make sure you first become friends with your costumer before asking for his email, so the likelihood of him ever coming back and buying is higher.

Be extremely friendly to your customers, if you are an unfriendly person be unfriendly to others, but not to your customers.

**Facebook**
Facebook is practically a mini-website of yours where you can introduce new products, interact directly with your customers, exchange contacts and information with them and listen to their feedback after a purchase.

You can start with the friends you already have on Facebook or you can create a page for your company, brand, product or service. Be sure to respond to comments and messages that your customers send and always leave contact information and how to locate your store or office.

**Whatsapp**
Nowadays there are whatsapp groups for everything and why not for you and your customers. Create a group where you regularly post product news, depending on the type of product you provide, post regularly but in a way that does not tire your customers.

**SMS**

If you've been in the habit of getting the phone numbers of your best customers, one way to keep in touch with them is by sending them messages when you have a new collection, a new product, a new shipment, and so on.

**Conclusion**
The secret of Relationship Marketing is to make friendships, be kind to your clients, ensure that you exist to solve their problems and not only to take their money, and be professional.
Do not overdo it mainly with forms of direct contact like SMS and whatsapp, be periodic and consistent, a good tip is to send information weekly or every two weeks.
Never push the customer too hard.

# Be Trustworthy

Okay so you know your product very well, you are persuasive, you know how people think and you treat people well and have a relationship with them. The only thing missing is trust. Your word should be your costumer's gospel. What you say about the products should hold true. Your products should stop working because the client misused them not because they are defective. And if they are defective you should be able to accept returns. You biggest aim should be to serve, serve, serve. Money is a byproduct of excellence in serving your costumers.

## Warranty or Risk Reversal

Offer guarantees, they can do wonders for your product or service. See the text below from the book: *Getting Everything You Can Out of Everything You Have Got* by Jay Abraham:

> The biggest secret to success in business or career is to always maintain the edge in everything you do. Logical sounding, yes, but infrequently understood. Even less frequently practiced. One of the biggest "competitive edge" advantages you'll ever gain is to always make it easier for the client to say "yes" than it is for them to say "no." You do it by taking away the financial, psychological or emotional risk factors that are always attached (stated or unstated) to virtually any decision-making proposition you ever ask a client to make. When you remove the risk for anyone deciding to do business with you it
> results in a powerful advantage in your business and financial success.
> (…)

An opal dealer I work with has a very daring guarantee: Anyone buying a stone from her takes it anywhere – to a friend, another jeweler, anywhere – and if they're dissatisfied, unhappy or just plain change their mind, it's no problem. They can get a full 100% money-back guarantee anytime within one year.

No other opal dealer in the country makes a claim like that. She outsells all her legitimate competition.

Risk reversal helps people decide to act and act now, today, immediately, without fear or concern.

(…)

When you start using risk reversal this way, your business almost always shoots up immediately and stays up. You close more sales, sell larger units of purchase and sell more often when people stop worrying about making the wrong or a bad purchasing decision.

When you use risk reversal, you are basically telling your client that they will never again make a bad or incorrect or dangerous purchasing decision. That's a powerfully persuading point to make.

## Your Credibility

A credible source of information makes for quicker and firmer decisions.

A credible person is expert (experienced, qualified, intelligent, skilled) and trustworthy (honest, fair, unselfish, caring). Charisma can increase credibility. Charismatic people, in addition to credible, are extroverted, composed and sociable.

Credibility is context-dependent, and an expert in one situation may be incompetent in another. It is also a cue that is used in selecting the peripheral route to decision-making.

How to Be Credible:

- Highlighting your own experience and qualifications.
- Showing you care about the other person and have their best interests at heart.
- Showing you are similar to them by using their language, body language, dress, etc.
- Being assertive. Quickly and logically refuting counter-arguments.
- Leveraging the credibility of others.
- Highlighting the credibility of your sources of information.
- Getting introduced by a credible person.

Be assertive when speaking to your costumers, language that reduces credibility includes:

- Ums, ers and other, ah, hesitation.
- Totally and absolutely excessive exaggeration.
- Kinds of qualifications that sort of lack assertion.
- Too much Politeness (that indicates subordination, be polite but not servile)
- I know it is silly to say this, but disclaimers do reduce credibility.

# So, How to Sell this Pen

This is not a long book, I told you at the beginning that if you want to know Marketing you should go to college, but to be a salesman you just need 5 things:
1. Know your product
2. Be Persuasive
3. Know how People Think
4. Treat Costumers Well
5. Be trustworthy

Our obsession with Marketing is clouding our judgment. Not everything needs a big marketing strategy to sell. Somethings just need good selling techniques.

Jotter Stainless Steel
Retractable Ballpoint Pen
With Chrome Trim Medium
Point

**$20.00**

So to Sell me this Parker Pen using everything you learned in this book. You wouldn't sell it to me right away.

You would
1. KNOW YOUR PRODUCT.
   You would research the crap out of this pen and not limit yourself to the small description. You would read the brochure, learn about all other Parker pens, learn about ballpoint pens in general and Parker's in particular. You would then study the competition and the pen industry in general, and come up with a favorable description of your own for this Parker pen, write it down and memorize it and train that description.
2. BE PERSUASIVE
   You would use persuasive techniques to convince me to buy the pen, like talk to me at ease like you are my best friend, call me by my name, show social proof if available, like how well this pen sells, who usually uses it, are they people like me? You would show your authority in this subject just by talking about it and guiding me, and you would show how in demand and scarce this pen is.
3. KNOW HOW PEOPLE THINK
   You could use so many cognitive biases to get me to buy the pen like the anchoring effect by showing me differently priced pens, one above and less good, and one very expensive.
4. TREAT COSTUMERS WELL

You would be having only my best interest at heart. Using all your knowledge about this particular pen and pens in general to serve me, to help me make the best decision, even if it means not selling me this pen but another one that is best suited to my line of work. And you would be having the time of your life doing that.
5. BE TRUSTWORTHY
   You would offer me guarantees, like telling me if the pen doesn't work, or suit me I could bring it back and get 100% refund. You would make me feel absolute sure of the pen.

THAT IS HOW YOU SELL THIS PEN.
You just need the Marketing of the Salesman.

www.ingramcontent.com/pod-product-compliance
Lightning Source LLC
Chambersburg PA
CBHW030512220526
45464CB00006B/2768